Medea's Cauldron

Deirdre Brennan

MEDEA'S CAULDRON

Medea's Cauldron

is published in 2022 by
ARLEN HOUSE
42 Grange Abbey Road
Baldoyle
Dublin D13 A0F3
Ireland
Email: arlenhouse@gmail.com
www.arlenhouse.ie

ISBN 978–1–85132–291–6, paperback

International distribution
SYRACUSE UNIVERSITY PRESS
621 Skytop Road, Suite 110
Syracuse
New York 13244–5290
USA
Email: supress@syr.edu
www.syracuseuniversitypress.syr.edu

Typesetting by Arlen House

cover image:
detail from 'The Sorceress' (1913) by J.W. Waterhouse

Contents

for all my grandchildren

Medea's Cauldron

Enheduanna (2285–2250 BCE)

Poet and hymnist, princess and priestess,
there you are in relief, sealed
to a translucent alabaster disk
overseeing a shaven-headed naked priest
pouring libations to the deity from a jug.

How your tall figure in a flounced dress
dominates the male priests at the altar,
your long black braided hair crowned
by a high rolled turban, the symbol
of your importance and influence.

I don't know when the storm bird nests
in the hulúppu tree outside your workplace window
but neither he nor his young are there today when I see you
again through the leaves, directing the business
of the city of Ur, its temple to the moon god, its radiance.

Nights in your Giparu Palace, you feed coals to the censer
releasing the sweet smell of frankincense and jasmine
as befits the coming of your divine muse
when you both become one in the elation of the word
that by morning in the temple the cantor will chant.

TIKTAALIK

Old fishapod, tetrapod, old fossil fish,
a biped in the making
give or take three hundred million years.
You had shoulders, elbows, wrists,
a neck moving separately from your body,
eyes on the top of your head.

I imagine you under a vermilion sun
among ammonites and coiled shellfish
in the brackish shallows
of a Devonian estuary using your hind fins
as feet and paddles to practise press-ups
on the unstable sedimentary floor

Nights come with a moon so close to earth
it almost fills your sky,
its brilliance quenching a muddle of stars;
rainstorms lash the shallows
where you embed your fins in the ground
in a tussle with the rush of the current.

Now trees are born, boles with thin roots
sprout small fernlike leaves.
You can pull yourself onto the bank,
feel your ribcage expand with air,
crawl on your fin-feet across the mudflats
and no birds shadow your skies.

Go between a fish and amphibian,
you were millennia ahead of the game
when we like you set foot on dry land,
no Aphrodites but ectopic things that chose
for safety to live in trees on leaves and berries
or crack molluscs on the shore.

Cashel Man

You lie naked and dead in the valley
under Crosy Duff Hill,
you, the young king who slept
between white linen sheets,
buffed the nails of your soft hands.
You, intercessor with the moody gods
of fertility failed to appease them
and they betrayed you in the end,
withholding rain for three seasons,
leaving you outcast by your angry people.

I hear the cries of your children on the wind,
see a henchman stab you in the neck,
another breaks your arm and when you are dead
they hack your spine in two and truss you up,
arms circling legs, knees towards your chest.
The mutilated body of a king, a buried offering
to the ever hungry gods, left for aeons
on a bed of sphagnum moss in Cashel bog,
a liminal place between two worlds.

You were unaware of the rhythms of nature,
the honking of swan and crane that sliced the skies,
the bittern's call from the reedbanks
and the acid bog water of the millennia that preserved
and tanned your skin brown as autumn leaves.
Nor did you hear the Bord na Móna milling machine
that unearthed your poor trussed body, one arm
pointing out of what was barely recognisable as a man.
Nor shall you know that the two sacred hazel stakes
that escorted you proclaimed your kingship.

December Moon

Step outside and look at the moon, they said,
but tired I went to bed and slept
with never a guess at her intent,
where she in her alignment with earth and sun
prised wide my eyes with a beam so intense
I moved like a dreamer to where she hung
low and bright above the casement window
fixing me with a mesmerist's fixed and steady stare.

Gone were the lava fields, her basaltic seas,
her radiance had quenched the stars,
outdazzled the show-off Geminid meteor showers,
tossed me like a bottle on a thousand tides,
veins running with rivulets of light,
my body vitreous, fragile and unknown,
a glassy Medusa afloat an eternal tide
sailing eastwards with her to meet the dawn.

The Glass Sky

Neither Titan, god of the stars,
nor Zeus, god of thunder and king of the sky,
with his retinue of debauched demigods
who tortured mortal men as a diversion
and ravaged their daughters,
ever dreamed of being dethroned
by a group of underpaid women
slogging at their desks on earth.

It was all at hand for them, sealed on the glass sky,
a boundless territory where old legends clung;
where seven hours a day they captured a host of stars,
split the light of each with prisms set in telescopes,
tried to made sense of our galaxy stretched before them,
decoded its caches of starlight, orbits of the planets,
and detached the Milky Way from Hera's cascading breasts
to reveal galaxy after galaxy in the unstoppable heavens.

They ignored the jibes of the men who referred to them
as Edward Pilkington's harem,
and the many who lamented
a lost paradise and the disenchantment of their night skies;
and not for the starwomen
the discordant music of the spheres
when they could hold the heavens in their laps,
a half a million photographs on glass plates
summonsing them,
fly-spankers in hand, to journey through stellar spaces
never before penetrated by human hand or eye.

Hibernation

Now the heart is a wintering butterfly
wings folded to a black triangle
wedged in the confines of time
that plays forfeits with us
pretending to give us the odds
and so much of that time already past.

My old apple tree, arthritic, misshapen,
knotted with swollen burls and ivy roots
wheezes in the January wind with never
a memory of ancestral apple woods
in the hills of the Tien Shan where black kites
soared above partridge and goldfinch.

We grow used to absences,
try to give faces and words to those
who have gone, the vanished parent,
the lost child. But we ourselves are lost
in the thickets of language, the blank
unknowingness of strangers.

Soul

Today I let your long-caged soul
loose on the wind,
watch it fly like thistledown
amongst gathering swallows
beneath a grey underbelly of cloud,
knowing it will never lodge
in a land where spores and sporelings
sleep the centuries, only to bud again
whenever they fancy the weather.

Your soul shelters in the last ray of daylight,
a gleam of floodwater at a field's edge,
the flame of a plunging kingfisher,
a drowned star deep in a water barrel.
And now, homing before autumn frosts
you are a linnet's breath on the window,
mindless of trees talking leaf to leaf,
the print of your life's narrative shrunken,
growing more faded by the day.

THE WITCHES

We are the crones, the witches,
the wise women who gathered healing herbs
in woods, meadows and thorn-brakes;
we are the ones who attended the childbed,
who swabbed festering ulcers and wounds,
who ground lady's bedstraw and larkspur
to dispel fevers, dysentery and sick joints.
We are the witches besmirched and vilified,
floated on waters to drown,
scapegoats burned at the stake.
Women like Hypatia of Alexandria, the astronomer
skinned alive by a rabble of crazed monks.

They said we were lascivious creatures,
unreasoning and opposed to reason;
they said we were familiars of the Devil
in order to gain power over men,
for they fear our sexuality,
our monthly blood, our forever yawning wombs.
They fear the threat of the belly heavy with child
without male reasoning in charge,
and they send their henchmen to stalk
and persecute us
until our ears fill with the crackling of kindling,
the smell of burning skin on the edge of memory.

Of Mice and Men

I never heard them steal in from winter,
the male, scaly-tailed eyes like black apple seeds,
leading his harem up the slopes of the pipe conduit
to a Mont Blanc of seldom-used blankets and sheets
piled on the teetering top shelf of the hot press.
I never heard them singing in the dark nights –
old songs of exile from Mesopotamia
muffled in rhythms of plumbing and shifting timbers;
tales of how their ancestors avenged the starving poor
and ate alive in his Mausethurm, the fat-cat
Bishop of Bingen who burned them to death in his barn.

It was spring when I climbed a ladder and found
the nesting place forsaken, the colony taken to the fields.
It stank of mouse; their urine and black droppings,
the bloodied bedclothes from the many litters born,
where safe from mouse trap and cat
they begot young ones again and again and again.

And I thought of Spiegelman's mice in another time,
scarcely daring to breathe in their hidey holes,
their shelter in safe houses betrayed, doors torn down
by cats in black jack-boots,
armed with guns and search lights.
I saw mice hanging in the town squares,
their hanging forms
becoming a language impossible to give words to,
mice injected with chemicals to glue shut their wombs,
hosed through freezing yards to the gas chambers,
shovelled as though they were rotten potatoes
into death pits.
I pick up soundings across an ocean of years,
the echo of the sentry cats' jokes still crack
in the compound.

The Vanished Ones

I see them in the shiver on the waters
where widgeon, teal and lapwing
winter on the flooded moors,
sense them on the amorphous land I walk
ill at ease with the shadows they cast.
They break boundaries of grass and stone
to ride windy spaces on a hill
and trail with will-o-the-wisp and spook lights
on the trembling bogs that entomb them.

Now I flee the dark of their yearning spirits
that shroud the scant grass paths
of this ghost grieving land,
the generic rocks that might be gravestones
and the conjoining roots of trees
where the bones of the raped and murdered
are layered bone upon bone
under the seep of the rain that washes them,
the sunrays that dry them.

Galileo's Other Daughter

For her no homecoming, no choice
but take the veil as her sister did,
sing the psalms and recite litanies
of prayers, all seven canonical hours of them
from chill matins and lauds to nones and vespers,
forever evading the father confessor's
roving hands.

She learned to live with poverty,
hunger pangs in the belly, the tedium
of days kneading bread, baking bread,
the endless laundry, sewing, lace making,
gathering bountiful herbs to blend the physic
to treat maladies and glean money
for the nuns' austere needs.

For her there was no coming to terms
with a father who wouldn't marry her mother,
a father whose indifference to his three children
saw them branded illegitimate in the baptismal files,
abandoning her and her sister with no chance of marriage,
for in the end it was invariably about him,
his stature, his genius.

She hankered after what might have been
had her father legitimised her, like her brother.
Imagined a loving husband, family, laughter and fun,
herself in the midst of them smiling, always smiling.
Instead, her mind and heart swelled with such darkness
she grew ill, took to the bed in mourning,
wearing her gloom
like a shroud.

The Wandering Womb

It's all a mistake the physician's talk
that I have this bestial thing within me,
a womb that doesn't accept its place,
breaks its tetherings with every moon change,
goes on a batter through my body squeezing
the lungs, bashing kidneys, liver and spleen,
beating its way to still my spinning heart.

Was it only yesterday I made daisy chains
in meadows of amaranthus and poppies,
wore amulets and powerful charms on wrist and
neck as a shield against a womb on the loose,
implored Athena, goddess of wisdom,
to deliver me from the diagnosis of physicians
who had made the womb their life's work.

And where is Athena now in my abandonment,
lying here in my hour of need where the sun swoons
outside the shuttered room and the physician has crushed
and bandaged my ribs to a breath-gasp,
barring the advance of the errant womb
he'll lure back to base with odours
of sweet wine, scented herbs and oil of roses
in the suppository he has rammed between my flanks.

The Beast God

You are a beast god towering over me,
your hide so white, so white.
But you don't smell of clovered meadows
as you stamp my skin with your hoof prints,
pound my breast bone till it snaps.
I am no Europa entranced by your allure
but a weakling with no art of morphing to a tree
sprouting laurel leaves for my defence,
and you leave me to founder
under your arsenal of stinging darts.

Waiting

There was no message, no sign of anyone after an hour
and she, fatigued by the waiting and the longing,
was dressed for home, lockers and presses checked
and double checked, wheelie luggage already at hand.

Inert as a heron in wait by a pool, she scanned the drive
for the car that would crawl to the entrance
to take her away,
her varicose veins after years of childbearing,
a ladder of stitches
encased like her feelings, in compressed stockings
of white spandex.

She never said goodbye or left the ward as I remember it.
Amidst the flurry of vacuum cleaners, polishers
and disinfectants
she must have slipped into the path of shadows,
never leaving as much as a print on the polished floor.

Stillbirth

All during spring, anxious
lest I lose a second of your life,
I swelled with bulb and bud,
the dizzy sap rising in me, your pulses echoing
in every hollow and harbour of my body.
I could hardly wait for you to lie in my arms.

I was astonished at how earthed you were,
how linked and bound to everything,
your face reflected in every pothole,
hair woven through white braids of clouds,
your eyes gazing at me
from the hearts of daisies,
the flame of your life like a fire
in the ribs of stone and leaf.

Had I been humming quietly,
crooning you lullabies
instead of singing lustily
at the top of my voice,
I would have noticed your retreat from me,
the way you fluttered like a sparrow
against the bars of a cage.
Too late I heard your death wail in my guts
echoing in the pulpy marrow of my bones.

They told me to take a photograph of you,
told me to look at you
when I didn't want to look, speak to you
when the talk would have been one-sided.
They told me to dress you in a white babygrow
when I had only ever planned to dress you
in purple or the saffron of the crocus.

These days it is the invisable things
that attract me,
the wren's nest, dark in the yew tree,
the map of roots clamping stone
and soil under the lawn,
the pull of underground rivers,
the treacherous riptides of my own body
that snatched you from me when I was off guard.

PORTENTS

Skeins of geese fly south,
a bite in the wind.
Another autumn comes.
Beet lorries on the road,
steam from the sugar factory
and me ankle deep in leaves.

I have just banished portents
I never sought or pursued
tripping me up in my path.
Are they giving me a warning
of death or bad weather?

Whether we like it or not
the old gods are with us still.
Don't be deluded about that.
They were merely taken down a peg or two
when driven out of the house.

They leave feathers like runic writing
on the thresholds of our doors.
Theirs are the gimlet eyes in the water
at the bottom of the *clais*, the snatch of song
that lies uneasily on the edge of hearing.

My threshold now snatched back, scrubbed clean,
feathers of the gods released to the winds,
I pretend I don't recognise their calling cards,
their lonely camouflage and concealment
with nobody to soft-soap them,
nor a whiff of incense to honour them.

Of Gods and Girls and Men

The old gods lived behind a gate of clouds,
took off with the speed of shooting stars
over air and water in their golden shoes,
feasted and caroused riotously
and basked in the frankincense
that billowed from countless altars
of human suppliants in the land below.

Yet there were times in their deathless state,
satiated with nectar, ambrosia and dulcet lyre,
beguiled by the goings-on of the earthbound,
they slipped into mortal lives disguised
as weary travellers to share a bacon stew,
take the form of swan, bull, or golden shower,
to make pregnant some lusted-after girl.

And what was that astounded maiden
hardly more than a child herself to make
of the celestial creature, half-man, half-bird,
emissary of a later god who eyed her from on high,
choosing that she of all mortals would bear his son
to unlock the gates of another world to men.
What could she do but nod a spellbound yes?

Athena

Tall and stately, helmet in hand,
she leans on a golden spear,
virgin goddess and protector,
clad head to winged heel
in her finely-pleated dress
of white pentelic marble,
peplos belted with snakeheads
and a snake embellished cape.

I see her divinity long ago defiled,
her nose bashed in, eyes gouged out
by holy men in black robes who rode
into Palmyra on tasselled mules
to talk the talk of their lord,
the one true male three-personed god
who would brook no strange gods
on earth or sky before him.

Down with goddesses. Down with Athena,
her wisdom, guidance, defence of the state,
its laws, its city walls and fortresses.
She who created the olive tree and plough,
taught folk to harness the oxen that pulled it,
inspired art, handcrafts and weaving,
stands scorned, a cross carved on her forehead,
her little owl on wide wings lost in the night.

THE NAZCA LINES

We stand here at the viewing point,
a platform high over a desert place
branded with marks of human possession,
triangles, trapezes, squares and spirals,
miles and miles of lines stretching away.

The aeons have neither erased nor blurred
the glyphic symbols of bird and insect,
monkey, owl-man, human hand and whale,
the paths incised so doggedly on the arid land
shining whitely between reddish pebbles.

Now those paths go on without their makers,
their star dances waver on every dawn. Echoes
of old chants to gods who dried their rivers, seared
their fields, ravened their bounty of human heads
like stray condors' feathers trying to wing it still.

Vigil

I wait on the beach,
see the plunge dive of cormorants,
the small black boat
speeding towards the reef.

Too far away to make out
the passengers leaving the boat,
you putting on your gear,
I picture you swimming with fish
amongst the red coral,
its tentacles so bright
reaching up to this blue day.

You floating in the shade
of its antlered arms,
in the quiet eddies
where sea urchins graze,
never see beyond the reef
a shiver of darker water
where the slim smooth-scaled
barracudas cruise.

RETREAT

You claw at wayward memories,
harvest lost times.
Faces long submerged surface,
old rugby teams, old scores.
Your span of life recedes
into your past,
leaving me behind.

Through an upstairs window
you watch the lime kiln stand
like a giant headstone
on the levelled-out site opposite,
your puzzled eyes searching
a ghost of the steam
that once mastered these skies.

The many voices of the river rise over you
like thistledown, like lark song,
a child's escaped red balloon.
Apples cool on the tree at evening
when your lungs are more at ease
but you are tired of waiting
and clouds crush you.

THE BLACK IRIS

You mustn't pick the wild black iris,
not that you had set your heart on it,
inky blooms, now black, violet, purple as evening
whose lustre will never light the walled gardens
of great houses or pampered suburban greenhouses,
for its home is emptiness and silence
where long ago travellers carved their names on rocks
and the wind sculpts pillars of stone to man and monster.

Eyes closed, you choose to be left behind
to dream whatever dreams you now dream
beside a pool where you don't swim anymore.
The world has grown tight around you.
Already you have gone beyond my reach
and the lure of a flower you mustn't pick.
Nightly you hear the djinn cry from the dunes,
marking time under a broken shard of moon.

Astray

A latch key to the French B&B
lets us into the hall,
a Stygian darkness
where no outlines, no shadows
guide the hand to a light switch.

My sightless eyes have lost you.
I call to you over a space
I don't dare to reach.
It is as if we have stepped
on the *fóidín mearaí*

that wandering sod of grass,
on which, if you walk,
you must drift in confusion
until the first rays of sunrise
set you free.

Somewhere water drips
as in a cave.
I strain to hear a boatman's oars
but the landlord appears
with much bonhomie in a glare of light.

Tonight we watch the ferryboat
slice the space between islands.
Ticket in hand you go aboard,
never once looking back,
and darkness swallows you.

No Words

We moved between knowing and not knowing,
so much said in the end, so much unsaid.
Months pass. Your face grows less clear.
Still no words will come for sorrow,
only the cry from the throat of a curlew,
the slow air from a plaintive flute.
Soon the clocks will go back. Another season
and the ground frosts that flank the heart.
But not for you the drifts of leaves,
your sloughed off days and nights at my feet.

This Autumn

These shortening days trigger changes in me
so that I shed the scales of my body
in tandem with falling leaves of birch and oak
and I cannot dodge the winds that dry the sap
to lay bare the shivering branch and bone.

Oh that my veins could be filled with the medicine
from Medea's cauldron of plants and roots, spices
and seeds, fox's heart and the pulp of mandrake
drawn shrieking from the earth, that will keep age at bay,
smooth out wrinkles, set pulses and heart to a new beat.

But now the skies are gravid and bruised with bitter rain
that will sweep away the scales and flakes of me
to swim with the brown rat in drains
and the shape shifting of this earth I know
will reshape to a cold cave, echoing with your absence.

The Ante Room

Day after day of galling rain,
great swollen drops, a sorcery on glass
that distorts the mountainous dunes outside,
the cut and trust of marram grass
on a land that seems bereft of any living thing,
where somewhere a listless tide drifts in and out
and no boat rides it.

We are in the ante room of death,
a place of whispers and shifting timbers,
for months now waiting in sallow light
like tired birds arrived in from the sea.
Our whole lives seem to have been directed
at this hour, this moment of dying
when the sky quenches its last streak of light.

The night nurse keeps a tactful distance.
She has timed the seconds each to each
until the one that stifles the thin song of life;
while somewhere a listless tide is on the turn,
the empty egg pods of ray and skate and shark
cast black lines along the length of shore
and an unseen boat has been and gone.

THE RUINED ABBEY

Under the endless moons and roofless years
the graves of the great and good
sink askew into the ruined abbey floor.
Frost fells the limestone grave slabs,
erasing the little histories of their lives.

And just because they were who they were
they could choose to hob nob in death
as close to the chancel as was fitting
with King Fedhlim, guarded by gallowglasses,
sceptred and crowned in his altar tomb.

Grave by grave we search out your people,
count how life by life became death;
their loves, ambitions, and pampered skin,
their rank and consequence shovelled under
in a flurry of incense and prayer.

We run fingers over a vortex of spent letters
that close the door on lives we might have dreamed:
the father who sowed his wild oats in Paris,
brought conch shells back from New Zealand,
the girl he loved still at a Belgian finishing school.

We pursue their daughters who rode to hounds,
sons killed and buried in the mud drifts of war,
their neighbours in Essex Lawn and Stony Park gone,
like the girl herself, her coffin on a hay float,
borne here to be buried when the hawthorn bloomed.

Uzes

We are in the old house, once a silk mill,
a mulberry tree by the door,
above us a stone tower and pigeonaire

whose nightly stirrings feather our sleep
and dawn wakens us
to stand in silence before its presence.

Days are quiet here, silk-screened to memory.
We sit on terraces where clingstones swell in pots
above gardens of pine and cicadas.

Evenings the men play boules in the yard.
We watch them scratch a circle in the grit,
throw the small wooden jack.

The women sit in chairs to watch the play,
listen to shouts, the hollow thump of boules,
both teams stooping to count their points.

But you are miles away, homing
to the curved bay and blurred playing fields
of youth where once you were king.

Light folds its wings and dives between trees.
You follow it to darkness
and I must tread on bird shadows to reach you.

Washing

Women were always washing clothes
in rivers and streams,
walloping them clean against rock and stone,
or up to the elbow
in suds, in big zinc baths with laundry boards
and Sunlight soap
each washday Monday devoted like a saint's day
to the chore.

My grandmother washed the bodies of the dead,
that duty too falling to a woman's care,
washed and shrouded she laid them out on her linen sheet
woven from flax that once grew blue as a summer's day
in their fields.

And when all was done, dead hands twined
with rosary beads, candles
placed at head and foot, she closed the window
through which the soul
had flown; tended to the drawing of curtains,
turned any mirrors
in the house to the wall and went home
to her seven children.

Back Then

The houses were cold back then.
Windows rattled in broken putty
and I had chilblains to the knee.

People began to die around town
and we visited corpses in white beds
on the way home from school.

We knew the houses of the dead
by the ruffled crepe bow on doors,
the black bordered cards marked RIP.

The priest said that we carried death
inside us even though we were young.
You had to be prepared to go

at a moment's notice or no notice at all.
No time to repent. We heard death's whisper
in convent chapels misty with incense.

Our skin goose-bumped with fear,
the priest gave us the magic letters
to trace on our foreheads before sleep.

I.N.R.I. *Jesus of Nazareth King of the Jews*
with the requisite aspiration *preserve me*
from a sudden and unprepared death.

Now that memories begin to recede
I have started to round corners of youth
with the illogic of a dreamer

and float through the improbable seasons
where days are agog with light,
creamy and warm, scrolling downwards

over streets, over rooftops that shift alignment
at each step I take and the known and unknown
pass me without as much as a glance.

The Botanist

i.m. Ellen Hutchins, 1785–1815

Here in the certitude of root and rising sap
she searched rootless things on rock and tree,
lichens, mosses, algae, brown, ochre and green,
the flowerless things that thrive in rain and fog –
adder's tongue, buckler, spleenwort
and horsetail whose airborne spores
rise like birdsong over evening.

Nights by lamplight in the silent house
she laid out one by one her plant trove,
tabled and classified the unclassified,
captured their perfection on paper
with fine brush and watercolour,
and moved by the marvel of discovery
shyly let some bear her name.

Today I think I see her figure ahead of me
on the shores and inlets she walked,
or through a screen of tangled roots and creepers
ahead of me again in the woods of Ardnagashel.
She is indistinct as moths that find shelter
in fissures of bark, or hide in lichens on an oak tree.
Her wings like theirs will never leave this place.

The Culling, March 2020

I see the culling of my generation
sitting in wheelchairs, lying in beds
in nursing and care homes,
scared and bewildered
by an invisible invader on a killing spree
through countries and continents,
rampaging at such a velocity
that in the space of a month
our world collapses around us.

Governments hold forth with many a spiel
of their priorities being the old and vulnerable,
but get diverted by more pressing concerns
that leave the aged and their carers abandoned,
begging for the help that never comes,
while Covid prowls their grim corridors,
snuffs out each smouldering wick of life.
And governments fudge the numbers of the dead
lest fear might turn to panic in the living.

I see the puzzled faces of my generation
try to understand a new language,
all acronyms, flattening curves and words
spelled as if to keep a child in the dark.
They are lost in a lockdown of solitude,
their too hasty deaths from the virus
put down to an underlying ailment;
and when they die, they die alone
without the solace of a loving hand to hold.

I'm old, very old, but I'm not an idiot!
With what vigour does the voice of centenarian
Maria Branyas from her care home in Spain
condemn the merciless indifference

of a dishonest society unmasked by Covid,
that banished the old to its margins a decade
before the pandemic when they lay soiled,
dehydrated, the skeleton staff in chaos knowing
the aged should not have to die like this.

I see the culling of my generation
in the photos of the dead who reach out to me
before the headlines and the evening news
who, now named and numbered, are set
afloat on so many commemorative wreaths
along brimming tranquillity pools
to the haunting lament of flute and uillinn pipes.
Tomorrow another set of sacrificial victims
will take their place,
and flute and uillinn pipes play on.

In Search of Meanings

We listen to oracles, bishops, moving statues,
search underworlds through lakes and caves,
only to get trapped, like Persephone,
in a no man's land, jammed somewhere
in the membranous conduits
between life and death, body and soul.

We look at others in lands
where people never leave this world,
join families round the fire at night,
work side by side with them in the fields,
dance at their weddings, and exhausted
return to their spirit houses to rest.

But here we are in search of meanings,
or the absolute meaning forever out of reach,
that tailing off like an animal's track in sand
doubles up on itself while our lives implode
like nascent stars returning to cosmic dust.

From what dark hole will we rise again
to seed the earth with the stuff of dreams?

The Witches of Ghana

They take their widowhood
to the witch camps,
their mood swings and menopauses,
their forgetfulness and dementia,
their outspokeness and loudness,
the evil spirits in their mouths,
for the chief and soothsayer branded
them the source of all illness, of death
and the drought that stalks the land.

This is their final submissiom to save
themselves from torture and lynching
by the men who coveted their houses,
their gardens of guavas and mangoes,
who swear they have intercepted curses
that have laid them prostate with backache,
malaria, and a wheeze in the lungs,
along with blinding them with a hail of arrows
hurled from the poisonous evil eye.

To be ageing women is a misfortune,
banished without a single possession
to lonely huts in the witch camp,
their stigamatised families unable to visit,
worried lest the only camp pump will run dry
and their tired feet never reach the river;
where day after day they watch the sky reel
with vultures, and at night the homing egrets
return to their roost in the trees.

FOXEARTH

We squeeze through a gap in the boundary hedge,
through a bastion of nettles and giant hogweed,
to a land that does not know us; where tussocks
of tangled grass send out suckers to trap us
and we hear no squawk of sentry jackdaw or rook,
no bird shriek to warn of our intrusion.

We have stumbled into an enchanted place,
free ourselves from low-lying branches of beech,
tread on the crackle of last year's leaves
to reach a clearance, an opening under oak roots,
the excavated earth kicked back to a half circle
where we whisper round the den of the king fox.

We have seen him stride across the lawn at dawn,
his red coat, slender muzzle, and bushy tail,
the upright ears that can hear a mouse stir.
Now he rests in cornfields where he has spent summer
waiting for his vixen's call back to fox earth
where she readies the birthing den for their spring cubs.

Shape changer. Keeper of a fabled pearl. Master of leaving
false trails. He will want all his skills to give the slip
to the hunters' guns, the howl of the hounds on the wind,
the lampers, their lights and dogs on a nightly spree.
But this is an enchanted place which they may never find,
or we, our whereness lost, may never leave.

The Little Rivers

Madlin, Ballyvaldin, Monefelim, Gowran –
these are the little rivers that run unseen
beneath bridges that span the new motorway.
You think of the thrust of them between reed beds
where mallard and moorhen nest,
morning mists ride the currents,
black moons in search of a reflection.

Here between rivers lepers sought refuge,
woke to ppriory bells cracking the dawn for matins,
dug their graves in the enclosure, tilled a garden,
and watched salmon swim upstream to spawn.
I hear their voices bead like water on ferns,
plummet to nettles and briar manes
that shroud the ruins of motte and bailey.

Now the wind has died in the gnarled *sceach*,
old byways and Mass paths grassed over,
holy wells deflected to drainage ditches
as the rivers sing of bridgeheads and heroes,
wild girls with roses in their hair who cast
their reflections in the flow like wishing coins
that never find the far side of a bridge.

FOREBODING

The mouth of the wind is sweet here
with hyssop, sage and lemon balm
but where is this place I find myself?
Somewhere I know or another?
The key I hold should turn in the lock,
open wide the door on a red-tiled hall.

I seem at home with these spaces around me
where light is dead and the dark beds down
like a drowsy watchdog one eye on guard.
But whose is the figure that stands in the window
that eats at my table and sleeps in my bed
who might be me, but isn't?

She has drawn all the curtains back.
I hear the scrape of an unseen name
engraved by a diamond ring on glass,
each letter an exorcism of what is me
echoing in rooms where angels
with lapis lazuli eyes stare at my passing.

Thoughts from an Ironing Board

I am ironing the angels' skirts
somewhat soiled from polluted skies;
no fallen angels these
nor fiery six-winged things
whose unclean feet
must lose themselves in feathers.

My angels wear shoes purple as heather
that covers the Killeshin hills.
Their wings like the wings of lacewings
never thundered with the roar of waterfalls,
nor have they brought coals to earth
from the altars of heaven.

They have served the generations well.
Long thin necks and eyes cast skywards,
they sing of past children who watched them
high in their tree-heaven of lights,
new children staring again in wonder,
and the old carried off on wings of the wind.

The Anatomy Museum, Harvard

I look into a long glass case
where gorgons to remove bladder stones lie,
trocars for the reduction of abdominal swelling,
surgical knives, forceps, lancets, needles,
and quite unlooked for I face the death mask of Burke,
plaster features untroubled, no rictus though hanged.

I imagine him and his accomplice, Hare,
stalking the alleyways of Edinburgh,
hunting lone victims for the anatomy table,
luring them to Hare's boarding house to be plied
with whiskey, strangled till they stopped breathing,
easier by far than prising open coffins in a cemetery.

They, on a roll, could never have envisioned Burke's end
on the gallows platform, legs bound, the hangman's noose;
a gala day for the multitudes, the balladeers, and hawkers,
the palpable hatred of the crowds baying for his blood,
cheering his every death twitch till his body was cut down
and they closed in like famished wolves to tear him apart.

THE NEW MOON AND DYING YEAR

The light wavers on the day's end
as if it would cling to the dying year.
I hunt the skies for the first new moon
in this auspicious January of two,
but over-young it does not appear
and no stars shine.

I see the mass of the rockery darkly,
the mossy rise of steps barely visible,
think of the high winds from the north
that will scour the quiet before dawn
and the shivering moon in her new boots
drawing the clouds around her.

In another time we walked the garden
treading soft snow under a full moon,
lit candles around the gazebo
that flamed unwaveringly till morning.
Now, no longer with me,
you belong to whatever eternity is.

The Clearance

It is late, dark enough to see the stars
as glassy as the moon that will quench them.
I have followed a thread of path through the woods
to a clearance between larch and birch,
a halting place for wolves when wolves loped the land,
a roosting place now for wintering owls.

And then I see a house rising before me
capped with branches and awnings of leaves
that fringe windows where faces in shadow look out.
A voice calls my name, a figure at the door beckons,
but if I step inside that door the wind will bang it shut
behind me and I will be held to ransom by spectres.

From Afar

I recognise each one clearly from afar,
the walkers and cyclists on this stretch of road,
their sense of whereness like bird feathers
winging the air currents after the bird has flown.

They are breaking the bounds if bounds there are
and like swallows that return to old nestings,
unerringly trace remembered flyways back
to close the distance between me and them.

But they belong to dead light, not this bright day,
for they sleep the sleep of the aeons now
with no earthly hours to span, yet part like a veil
some shifting curtain of air that lets them through

with no attempt whatever at disguise,
and being shades it is hard to see
how they are not erased by light
but the sudden blink of a double take.

Caged Men Watch Birds

Caged men watch colours change
in the valley,
an outline of hills floating away,
the flutter of birds to the barbed-wire fence,
their sudden sallies after winged insects.

Life is debased,
flea and louse-ridden.
Days and years chug past,
prisoners shot dead on a guard's impulse,
men taking their own lives.

Caged men beguiled by birds
stare outwards,
join migrant rooks and jackdaws
in the fields,
nest with redstarts in tree holes,
trail with them along hedges and streams.

Caged men when free are forever caged,
but for times in sleep
dreaming a rumpus of redstart and finch
on a barbed-wire fence they fly
like birds themselves
feather, muscle and pinion straining.

The Red Dancers

In cave after sea cave the dancers
dance themselves to a balletic trance,
stick-figures painted in blood-red haemetite
crushed to powder and mixed to a paste
with rain water, spittle and clay.
Torch light plays on the cavorting revellers
giving an illusion of movement
to legs splayed wide in split-leaps,
arms gliding like the wings of sea eagles
across the polished granite walls.

Windborne through the generations,
an old music comes and goes in a flurry
of tuneless notes blown on holes punched
in the hollow leg bones of gulls,
the rhythm of drum beat, hand clapping
and clack of stone castanets that sets
the dancers' feet adance; while staff in hand
the Shaman, high on his ritual drink,
invokes their deities to guide their harpoons
to elk meat, their boats to offshore seals.

The Last Dance

When I heard that death had taken you
I wondered if he had come to call as before
in the guise of that Latin American revolutionary
who whirled you from the hospital bed where you lay
so ill, and danced you down his wild corridors
to the pulsating beat of chacarera and rumba.

After all that spinning, and you half in love with him,
your head dizzy as a drowning willow in a river's spate,
a spirogyra of stars in a far constellation,
he suddenly jilted you, abandoning you with sangfroid
in a breathless state hitched to tubes and drips
and the doctors who had fought him for your life.

Now decades later hearing that I have lost you forever
I think of you ignoring a lineup
of Holbein's skeletal dancers
as you lay claim to the last dance
with your Latino revolutionary
who awaits you in olive fatigues,
beret and laced up military boots.
Pain slips like a silk shawl from your shoulders and I see
the infinitudes of your being scatter in the insatiate dance.

Midsummer's Eve

Eve of night moths and will-o'-the-wisps,
festival of fires as old as Baal, an apt time
for me to cremate you or what remains of you
in your coffin case at the back of the garage.
My garden barrow, your catafalque,
I wheel you ceremonially along the gravel path
to the burial pyre you sought but didn't get.

I never thought to bring you on this ritual walk
under an apricot evening sky that shuts out spectres,
place you on a bed of elder flowers and herb vervain
such as Solomon used to cleanse his temple,
align you east to face the rising sun
then long match in hand set your coffin case ablaze
and feed your grave clothes in

and the white suit of which you were so proud
takes a leap upwards whether in exultation
or protest is hard to say but I stay with you
until there is nothing left when the ashes stir
but memories of our shared childhood.
And in the morning when the ground is cool
I plant a daffodil in you.

Enheduanna

Enheduanna (c. 23rd Century BCE, Mesopotamia) is the world's first known author. Her work – a collection of hymns written in cuneiform on calcite discs – was discovered by the archaeologist Charles Leonard Woolley in 1927 when excavating the ancient Sumerian city of Ur. Her poetry is inscribed with her name and the words by which she laid claim to her work: *'My king, something has been created that no one has created before'*. The lunar calcite disc referenced in the first stanza of *Enheduanna* is in the Penn Museum (University of Pennsylvania), the collections of which can be explored digitally. My thanks to Adam Falkenstein and Roberta Binkley for introducing me to the importance of Enheduanna's work through their research and writing.

The Glass Sky

Known as the 'Harvard Computers', a team of skilled women processed astronomical data in the Harvard Observatory under the direction of Edward Charles Pickering from 1877 to 1919 and, following his death in 1919, by Annie Jump Cannon. Dava Sobel tells their story in *The Glass Universe: how the ladies of the Harvard Observatory took the measure of the stars* (Viking, 2016).

Fly-spanker: a small glass plate on which are images of stars of different brightness.

Of Mice and Men

Art Spiegelman's *Maus* (Pantheon Books, 1991, previously serialised 1980–1991) was nominated for the National Book Critics Circle Award and won the Pulitzer Prize in 1992.

Stillbirth
Translated by the author from her original poem in Irish, *Marbhghin* (*Wild Pulses,* Arlen House, 2017).

Some of these poems or versions of them have been published previously by *Poetry Ireland, The SHOp, The Irish Times, Literary Review, Her Other Language.*

I am grateful, as always, to Alan Hayes, of Arlen House who has published my work over the past 20 years.

Once again, my heartfelt thanks to Niamh Brennan for her untiring support with the compilation of each of my books.